AI-Era Social Network: Reimagined for Truth, Trust & Transformation

Paramendra Kumar Bhagat
www.paramendra.com

Table Of Contents

A social network purpose-built for the **Age of AI**—and **designed to mitigate the harms of misinformation**—would look and function very differently from today's platforms. Here's a comprehensive vision for what it might be:

🌐 AI-Era Social Network: Reimagined for Truth, Trust & Transformation

1. Foundational Philosophy: Design for Integrity

- **Human flourishing as the core metric**, not engagement or profit.

- Built to **enhance critical thinking, social cohesion, and civic discourse**, not manipulate attention.

- **Algorithmic transparency** and **ethical AI** as guiding principles.

---

2. Key Features & Innovations

⬛ AI-Assisted Truth Layer

- Every post (text, image, video) is run through a **real-time fact-checking AI** using multiple verified sources.

- Labels appear when:

    - A claim is **contested**, **false**, or **outdated**.

    - A post uses **AI-generated content**.

- Claims can be traced back to **source data**, with citations.

💬 Contextual Commenting

- Comments are ranked not by likes, but by **constructive contribution**, **civility**, and **informational quality** (judged by hybrid AI + community upvotes).

- "Smart Comments" summarize diverse opinions using AI for users who want the TL;DR.

🤖 Personal AI Assistant

- Each user has a **custom AI companion** that curates content, explains difficult ideas, helps spot misinformation, and can debate you for fun or understanding.

🔒 Data Ownership & Privacy

- You own your data. You can export, delete, or monetize it on your own terms.

- Zero hidden tracking. No selling user behavior to third parties.

🧠 Bias-Aware Algorithms

- AI feeds are calibrated for **ideological diversity** and **worldview expansion**—not echo chambers.

- You can toggle modes: "Challenge Me," "Balance Me," or "Comfort Me."

● Verified Identity + Pseudonymity Zones

- Real-name verified zones for **public discourse** (debates, townhalls).

- Pseudonymous areas for **creativity, vulnerable expression, or dissent**.

- No bots or fake accounts—**AI bot detection runs in real-time**.

✏ Civic Labs & Feedback Loops

- Users can opt into **"social experiments"** like upvote-free feeds or idea-swapping challenges.

- Continuous **A/B testing of new norms**, reviewed by a **Citizen Ethics Panel**.

---

3. Building It: Key Principles for Construction

🗿 Interdisciplinary Core Team

- AI engineers + ethicists + sociologists + journalists + psychologists.

- Advisory board includes former misinformation researchers, educators, and civil rights leaders.

⚖️ **Decentralized Infrastructure**

- **Federated architecture** (like Mastodon) allows for local governance.

- Smart contracts govern moderation rules in transparent, auditable ways.

■ **Monetization without Manipulation**

- Revenue from:

    - **Optional subscriptions** (ad-free, premium tools).

    - **Micropayments for high-quality content** (think: Patreon + Medium).

    - **Public grants** for civic innovation (as part of digital infrastructure).

---

4. Positive Impacts on Society

- Becomes a **learning tool**, not just a scrolling trap.

- Acts as a **digital public square**, promoting **civil dialogue**.

- Fosters **media literacy**, **resilience to manipulation**, and **cross-cultural empathy**.

- Builds **institutional trust** by showing how claims are verified.

---

5. Sample Use Case

Imagine this:

> You're reading a post about a new climate bill. Your AI assistant flags that a statistic cited is outdated and shows you 3 alternative sources. You ask your assistant to "show me conservative and liberal takes on this," and it gives you a two-minute summary from both sides. A comment thread below has been AI-sorted, prioritizing thoughtful replies and diverse views. You click to join a Civic Lab experiment testing how people respond when comments have no usernames—just ideas.

"The Next Social Network: Reimagining Human
Connection in the Age of AI"

📚 Book Outline: 12 Chapters

Chapter 1: The Collapse of Trust

- How traditional social networks amplified division, misinformation, and emotional manipulation

- The engagement economy and its unintended consequences

- Why the current system is unsustainable

Chapter 2: Anatomy of Misinformation

- How misinformation spreads and why it works

- Case studies: pandemics, elections, wars

- The psychological and algorithmic roots of virality and polarization

---

Chapter 3: A New Social Philosophy

- Designing for truth, dignity, and connection—not attention

- Civic health as the north star metric

- Lessons from public infrastructure, journalism, and science

---

Chapter 4: Building the AI Truth Layer

- How AI can fact-check, verify, and contextualize content in real time

- Building a multi-source knowledge engine

- Limitations of current LLMs and solutions for hallucination and bias

---

Chapter 5: AI Companions, Not AI Puppeteers

- Giving users personal AI assistants for knowledge, safety, and dialogue

- Use cases: AI for debate, translation, mental health, and information hygiene

- The ethics of personalized AI agents

Chapter 6: Designing for Healthy Dialogue

- Replacing like counts with constructive feedback loops

- AI-sorted comment sections and misinformation scoring

- Encouraging humility, curiosity, and reflection

Chapter 7: Escaping the Echo Chamber

- Algorithms for worldview expansion and ideological diversity

- Modes like "Challenge Me" and "Balance Me"

- Case studies in depolarizing design

Chapter 8: Identity in the Digital Age

- Real identity vs pseudonymity: striking the right balance

- Bot detection, sybil resistance, and the end of troll armies

- Verified zones for civic discourse, anonymous zones for safety

Chapter 9: Infrastructure for Integrity

- Federated social networks, data sovereignty, and user governance

- Web3 and decentralized identity tools

- A transparent, auditable moderation and governance model

Chapter 10: Monetizing Without Manipulation

- Moving beyond ads and surveillance capitalism

- Subscription models, micropayments, and public interest funding

- Aligning financial incentives with civic outcomes

Chapter 11: Civic Labs and Ethical Experimentation

- Prototyping new digital norms in real time

- A/B testing for the public good

- How to run ethical social experiments with user consent

Chapter 12: The Future of Digital Society

- What a better social internet looks like

- How next-gen social networks can rebuild trust, foster empathy, and power democracy

- A call to action for technologists, founders, and citizens

Chapter 1: The Collapse of Trust

In the first two decades of the 21st century, the world witnessed a digital transformation unlike anything in human history. Billions of people came online, connected across continents, shared photos, jokes, political opinions, and personal milestones in real-time. Social networks promised a new era of democratized information, global dialogue, and participatory culture. For a while, it seemed utopian.

But then the cracks began to show.

What started as platforms for connection quietly became engines of division. Behind the colorful interfaces and friendly "like" buttons was a business model based not on trust or truth—but on attention. In this new economy, outrage was currency. The more emotional a post, the more likely it was to be shared. The more divisive a headline, the more valuable it became. Algorithms optimized not for accuracy or nuance, but for engagement. And engagement thrived on conflict.

The rise of misinformation wasn't an accident. It was a byproduct of incentives.

The Crisis of Information Overload

When everyone became a broadcaster, the line between journalism and opinion blurred. Fact-checkers couldn't keep up with meme machines. Photoshopped images, deepfakes, and synthetic media created a hall of mirrors where even the most discerning users struggled to tell real from fake. Meanwhile, conspiracy theories—once relegated to the fringes—found fertile ground in algorithmically fueled echo chambers.

Trust in institutions collapsed. Trust in each other did, too.

Elections were compromised. Vaccines became battlegrounds. Science, long a shared foundation for truth, was reframed as ideology. The problem wasn't just fake news—it was that **people no longer agreed on what a fact even was.**

A Generation Born Into Doubt

For young people raised in this climate, distrust became default. Every tweet might be a trap. Every headline might be bait. Every photo might be AI-generated. As technology advanced, so did skepticism. And rightfully so. Bots masqueraded as humans. Troll farms gamed comment sections. Influencers sold authenticity by the pound.

The internet had democratized speech—but without any system of verification, quality, or care, it also became a digital Wild West. The result: **a society more connected than ever, but more fragmented, anxious, and hostile than before.**

The Engagement Dilemma

Major platforms repeatedly promised reform—stronger content moderation, independent fact-checking, algorithmic transparency. Yet their core business models remained unchanged. The longer you stayed scrolling, the more they profited. Misinformation wasn't a glitch. It was a feature. To change the system would mean questioning the very foundation of modern tech capitalism.

Few dared.

In the meantime, real-world consequences mounted. Genocides were incited on Facebook. Democracies wobbled under the weight of disinformation campaigns. People died because they believed lies they read on Reddit or YouTube.

This wasn't just about bad actors. It was about the **design** of the networks themselves. Platforms weren't neutral. They shaped reality—what we saw, what we believed, who we trusted.

And trust was running out.

A Fork in the Digital Road

The collapse of trust was never inevitable. It was the result of choices: choices about metrics, incentives, design, and governance. But those choices can be undone—and better ones can be made.

This book is a blueprint for a new kind of social network. One that learns from the failures of the past and embraces the possibilities of AI, not as a manipulative force, but as a tool for clarity, truth, and deeper connection. One that treats trust as the product—not the collateral damage.

Because in the age of AI, it's no longer enough to connect people.
We must connect them wisely.

Chapter 2: Anatomy of Misinformation

To build a better social network, we must first understand the architecture of the problem. Misinformation is not just the result of people lying online. It's a systemic, multi-layered issue deeply rooted in psychology, technology, and the economics of attention.

The misinformation crisis is not simply about "bad facts." It's about **how information spreads**, **why we believe what we do**, and how algorithms amplify messages in ways that humans can't predict—let alone control.

Let's dissect it.

The Psychology of Belief

Humans are not rational creatures. We are pattern seekers. Tribal. Emotional. We gravitate toward information that confirms what we already believe—a cognitive bias known as **confirmation bias**. When we encounter something that contradicts our worldview, our first instinct is not to reconsider—it's to reject, rationalize, or attack.

Social networks supercharged this tendency. Instead of a slow, reflective news cycle, we entered an era of **instant reaction**. Nuance lost to speed. Emotion won over evidence.

And it turns out, false information travels farther, faster, and deeper than the truth.

A 2018 study by MIT found that **falsehoods were 70% more likely to be retweeted than the truth**. Why? Because they're often more surprising, emotional, or sensational. "Obama born in Kenya" gets more attention than "Obama releases birth certificate."

In short: **what feels true often beats what *is* true**.

The Algorithmic Megaphone

At the core of every social platform is an invisible architect: the algorithm. It decides what you see. It rewards what gets clicked. And it learns quickly what keeps you scrolling.

But the algorithm doesn't know fact from fiction. It doesn't know hate from humor. It optimizes for one thing: **engagement**.

And that's the problem.

If an incendiary lie generates more engagement than a boring truth, the algorithm amplifies the lie. Over time, entire feeds are shaped by what provokes, not what informs.

These aren't bugs. They're **design decisions**.

From Fringe to Feed

Before social media, fringe beliefs struggled to break into mainstream discourse. A flat Earth society might print pamphlets or hold small meetings. Today, they can post a viral video and instantly reach millions.

The distance between fringe and mainstream has collapsed. Extremist content no longer sits at the edges—it now **thrives in the center** of the conversation.

In fact, some of the most egregious misinformation campaigns—QAnon, anti-vaccine propaganda, election denialism—didn't just spread in spite of social media. They spread *because* of it.

The Weaponization of Doubt

Misinformation isn't just spread by accident. Increasingly, it's weaponized deliberately.

State actors, organized troll farms, and ideological extremists have learned how to game the system. They plant seeds of doubt, manipulate hashtags, and swarm comment sections—not to promote one truth, but to blur the line between truth and lies entirely.

Their goal isn't just to persuade you. It's to **confuse you**—to make you question everything until nothing feels reliable. That's the true cost of misinformation: a society where consensus becomes impossible and collective action breaks down.

Platforms in Denial

For years, social media companies downplayed their role. They argued they were merely platforms, not publishers. They claimed neutrality while profiting from controversy.

Eventually, they acknowledged the problem—but too often their solutions came too late, or were superficial. A fact-check label. A warning banner. Temporary account suspensions. All helpful, but not nearly enough.

Because the rot was deeper. It wasn't just in the content—it was in the design of the systems themselves.

Lessons Learned

From Myanmar to Michigan, we've now seen what happens when misinformation spreads unchecked. Ethnic violence. Vaccine resistance. Attacks on democratic institutions. These are not abstract concerns. They are **real-world consequences** of digital negligence.

The lesson is clear: **Information environments shape human behavior.** And if we don't shape those environments with care, others will shape them with malice.

We can no longer treat misinformation as an unfortunate side effect. It is **the defining design challenge of our time.**

If we are to build a social network for the Age of AI, we must treat truth not as optional—but as foundational. That means rethinking everything: how we rank posts, how we reward engagement, how we verify claims, and how we empower users to discern for themselves.

In the next chapter, we begin that work—with a new social philosophy that puts trust, truth, and human dignity at the core.

Chapter 3: A New Social Philosophy

The social web needs a soul.

For far too long, social networks have been designed to exploit our instincts, not elevate our intellect. They've optimized for clicks, not character. They've measured success in hours spent, not minds changed. The result has been a networked society that is more connected, yet more divided, distracted, and distrustful.

It doesn't have to be this way.

If we are to build a social network for the Age of AI—one that becomes a **net positive for society**—we must root it in a radically different set of values. This chapter explores the **philosophical foundation** of that vision.

The Core Question: What Is This For?

When you strip away the ads, algorithms, and avatars, a social network is, at its core, a system for **mediating human relationships**. It determines:

- What we see

- Who we hear

- How we speak

- What gets rewarded

Which means it shapes **what we value**, **how we think**, and even **who we become**.

The question isn't whether a social network has a moral impact—it's **what kind of moral impact** it has.

From Extraction to Empowerment

The dominant model of the last two decades has been **extractive**: extract attention, extract data, extract value from users to serve advertisers. This model treats people as **resources**, not as citizens, thinkers, or creators.

A new social philosophy must be **empowering**: help people understand more, express more meaningfully, connect more honestly, and grow more intentionally.

This means designing **for the user's well-being**, not their compulsive engagement. It means building networks that ask not, "What keeps them here?" but "What helps them grow?"

The Three Pillars of the New Philosophy

A next-generation social network must rest on three philosophical pillars:

1. Truth as a Systemic Goal

Truth must be **baked into the system**, not patched on afterward. That means:

- Prioritizing verifiable information

- De-prioritizing proven falsehoods

- Promoting epistemic humility (the awareness of what we don't know)

The platform doesn't need to act as the final arbiter of truth—but it should act as an **intelligent guide** that makes truth easier to find and falsehoods harder to spread.

2. Dignity by Design

Every interaction—whether posting, commenting, or debating—should be governed by respect for human dignity. That means:

- Tools that encourage empathy and reflection

- Guardrails against harassment and abuse

- UI/UX that encourages listening, not just shouting

A dignity-first design protects the **vulnerable**, uplifts the **thoughtful**, and restrains the **malicious**.

3. Community Over Virality

Today's platforms reward **scale and spectacle** over intimacy and depth. A better network would shift toward:

- Smaller, meaningful interactions

- Group-based trust systems

- Localized, interest-based, or civic-centered communities

The goal is not global reach, but **authentic resonance**.

Inspired by Public Infrastructure

A useful analogy is the public square. A well-designed public square invites dialogue, promotes coexistence, and reflects the values of the society that built it.

We don't build roads that lead into traffic jams or parks that provoke fights. We shouldn't design social platforms that do.

Imagine social media treated as **public infrastructure**: held to standards of accessibility, transparency, and social utility. Not a Wild West, but a digital city with zones for art, education, civic debate, and quiet reflection.

This is not to say the network must be government-run. Rather, it should **adopt the civic mindset**: a commitment to the common good.

Digital Rights and Responsibilities

A new philosophy also requires a new **social contract**—a clear articulation of what users can expect, and what is expected of them. This could include:

- The right to control your data

- The right to transparency about how content is ranked

- The right to contest decisions made by AI

- The responsibility to engage in good faith

- The responsibility to report harm and protect others

In short: **citizenship in the digital age.**

AI as Steward, Not Sovereign

We must also be clear about the role of AI. AI should not replace human judgment, but **augment it**. It should not manipulate people, but **support their autonomy**.

An AI-augmented social network might:

- Provide context and counterpoints to posts

- Flag false or manipulative content

- Translate ideas across languages and cultures

- Protect users from harassment and fraud

But it should always be **accountable, auditable, and user-directed**.

Toward a Flourishing Society

The ultimate goal of any great social system should be **human flourishing**. Not just survival. Not just convenience. Flourishing.

A social network built on this foundation wouldn't just reduce harm—it would actively do good:

- Elevate critical thinking

- Inspire curiosity

- Strengthen relationships

- Promote civic engagement

- Nurture empathy

- Encourage creativity

It would not be a platform we escape to—but a tool we return to **with purpose**.

The Journey Ahead

Philosophy alone is not enough. We need design principles, technologies, governance models, and business incentives that bring these ideals to life.

In the next chapter, we begin with the most critical feature of all: a **truth layer**—a system that ensures what we see is as close to reality as possible in a world of infinite manipulation.

Because truth is not a luxury.
 In the age of AI, it is a **requirement for survival**.

Chapter 4: Building the AI Truth Layer

In a world where synthetic media can be generated with a single prompt, truth becomes fragile. Images can be faked. Voices can be cloned. Articles can be fabricated by machines. As AI becomes more powerful, so does the capacity to deceive. And so, any social network built for the AI era must prioritize a bold, systemic solution:

It must build a **truth layer.**

This truth layer is not a single fact-checking tool or a moderation team buried in a corporate basement. It is a real-time, AI-powered infrastructure that evaluates, contextualizes, and enhances every piece of content that enters the network. It is **always on**, **transparent**, and **trusted**.

The Truth Layer Defined

A truth layer is an intelligent system that overlays digital content with **contextual metadata**. For any post—whether a news article, video, meme, or comment—the truth layer provides:

- **Source tracing**: Where does this claim come from? What is its origin?

- **Credibility score**: How reliable is the source according to independent standards?

- **Claim verification**: Is the factual content supported by data or debunked by evidence?

- **Opposing viewpoints**: What are other credible perspectives on this issue?

- **AI flagging**: Is this image, video, or text AI-generated or manipulated?

In short: It doesn't tell you **what to think**, but it gives you the **tools to think better**.

Why the Existing Model Fails

Current platforms attempt to combat misinformation with retroactive moderation—flagging or removing content *after* it goes viral. But by then, the damage is done.

Moreover, human fact-checkers are outnumbered and outpaced. Every minute, thousands of posts are uploaded. No team—no matter how skilled—can scale fast enough.

Only AI can meet this challenge. But it must be **intelligent AI**—fed by trustworthy sources, guided by human values, and designed for **assistance, not control**.

How the Truth Layer Works

Let's imagine how it functions, moment to moment:

Step 1: Ingestion

As a user posts content, the system immediately scans it. Is it text, image, video, or audio? AI models begin analyzing for factual claims, media authenticity, and source attribution.

Step 2: Real-Time Verification

If a factual claim is detected, it is run against a distributed knowledge graph built from:

- Peer-reviewed research

- Reputable news organizations

- Government and NGO databases

- Fact-checking networks

- Crowd-verified sources with reputation scores

AI cross-references these sources and assigns a **probabilistic truth value**, with explainability built in.

Step 3: Augmented Display

Instead of removing content, the system **augments it**:

- ■ Verified claims are highlighted with green check marks and source citations

- ▲ Disputed claims carry a context warning and links to counter-sources

- ✖ Debunked falsehoods are overlaid with a clearly visible flag

All this happens in real-time, before the content spreads.

Step 4: User Interaction

Users can click for deeper insights: timelines of how the claim spread, comparison with similar narratives, or even **a visual map of opinion clusters**.

They can also report new issues, contribute source links, or vote on trustworthiness—training the system over time.

Detecting Synthetic Media

With generative AI producing increasingly realistic fake content, the truth layer must also be a **forensics engine**. It uses:

- **Reverse image search and pixel anomaly detection**

- **Audio watermarking and voiceprint analysis**

- **Text stylometry** to identify AI-generated writing

- **Blockchain-backed content signing** from trusted creators

The goal is not to ban synthetic content but to **label it**—so users always know what's real, what's synthetic, and what's ambiguous.

Challenges and Limitations

No system is perfect. The truth layer will face:

- **Gray areas**: Not all claims can be conclusively proven or disproven

- **Bias risks**: Which sources get prioritized, and whose truth gets amplified?

- **Manipulation**: Bad actors may try to flood the verification system with false flags or credible-looking disinformation

- **Speed vs accuracy**: How to balance rapid response with thoughtful analysis

That's why **human oversight** remains essential. The AI truth layer should operate like a **first-responder**, while expert moderators, journalists, and civic panels act as the **judicial review**.

Radical Transparency as Trust-Building

To avoid becoming a black box, the truth layer must be:

- **Open source**: Anyone can inspect how it works

- **Audit-friendly**: All claims and scores are timestamped and traceable

- **Participatory**: Users can suggest improvements, challenge scores, and help train the AI

This kind of transparency turns users from passive consumers into **co-curators of the truth**.

A Paradigm Shift

The AI truth layer represents a shift from **content moderation** to **content contextualization**.

It respects free speech—but also empowers **informed speech**. It doesn't silence dissent—but ensures dissent is grounded in reality. It turns AI from a source of manipulation into a **guardian of discernment**.

Imagine if, instead of a battlefield of opinions, your social feed became a **living encyclopedia**—dynamic, contested, but guided by structure and care.

That's the promise of the truth layer.

The Next Step

With truth infrastructure in place, we can turn to the second great challenge: **human interaction**. Because information alone isn't enough—we need a space for **dialogue, disagreement, and mutual understanding**.

In the next chapter, we'll explore how to redesign **comments, conversation, and community** for the AI age—so that online discourse doesn't devolve into chaos, but evolves into something **worthy of our better nature**.

Chapter 5: AI Companions, Not AI Puppeteers

In the early 2020s, artificial intelligence made a dramatic leap. Language models could now write essays, simulate conversations, compose songs, and even pass standardized tests. AI-generated avatars offered companionship, advice, and emotional support. Chatbots began to answer questions better than search engines.

Suddenly, every person online had access to a level of intelligence that once required a team of researchers—or at least a very patient librarian.

But with this new power came a dilemma:
 Would AI serve us as companions—or control us as puppeteers?

This chapter explores the role of **personal AI agents** in the next-generation social network—not as manipulative forces nudging us toward clickbait, but as **trusted allies** guiding us toward clarity, empathy, and better decisions.

From Feed to Dialogue

Traditional social media is largely a one-way street: the algorithm decides what you see; you react. It's passive consumption dressed up as interaction.

In an AI-powered network, the experience becomes **dialogical**. You no longer just scroll—you **converse**. With your feed. With your content. With your own personalized AI guide.

Imagine reading a heated political post. Your AI companion could:

- Summarize the key claims and rate their factual reliability

- Provide counterarguments from respected thinkers on all sides

- Help you understand the emotional manipulation tactics at play

- Suggest a civil way to enter the conversation—or advise you to disengage

In other words, your AI doesn't tell you what to think. It helps you **think better**.

Meet Your AI: Roles and Capabilities

A next-gen social network could offer each user an **AI Companion** that performs multiple helpful functions:

🧠 Cognitive Assistant

- Summarizes long articles, threads, and videos in seconds

- Answers clarifying questions

- Highlights biases, fallacies, or manipulative language

- Suggests deeper research paths based on your curiosity

💬 Dialogue Coach

- Encourages thoughtful phrasing in comments

- Helps de-escalate arguments with empathy prompts

- Translates ideas across worldviews

- Flags when you may be reacting emotionally, not thoughtfully

● Perspective Broadener

- Recommends voices from different geographies, ideologies, and identities

- Surfaces underrepresented viewpoints on current issues

- Creates dynamic "worldview maps" of trending debates

🧘 Emotional Companion

- Checks in on your emotional health during online sessions

- Helps detect signs of burnout, agitation, or doomscrolling

- Suggests breaks, wellness tools, or calming content

This is **not a replacement for therapy** or human connection. But it is a tool that can help restore **balance, awareness, and intentionality** in an overwhelming online environment.

The Line Between Help and Manipulation

With great cognitive power comes great ethical responsibility.

The AI companion must be built on principles of **agency, transparency, and user control**. That means:

- It never nudges you without consent

- It explains its reasoning and suggestions

- You can customize its tone, values, and areas of focus

- You can turn it off or switch to alternative models

Importantly, the AI is **not monetized through behavioral data**. Its incentives must always align with your well-being—not with advertisers or engagement metrics.

Training Your AI

Each user's AI would improve over time—not to trap you in a filter bubble, but to **understand your learning style, your tone preferences, and your blind spots**.

You could even **train your AI on your favorite thinkers**, upload readings you care about, or adjust "challenge settings" to expose yourself to unfamiliar or opposing ideas.

It becomes **a partner in your growth**, not a mirror for your ego.

Shared AI Experiences

In addition to private companions, the platform could offer **shared AI tools**:

- In group chats, AI could offer neutral summaries of arguments

- In comment threads, it could highlight common ground between polarized users

- In civic forums, it could generate collective summaries or proposals based on public input

This is AI not as a gatekeeper—but as a **facilitator of deeper conversation**.

Creative Possibilities

Beyond logic and debate, AI companions could also assist with:

- **Creative expression**: helping you write, draw, brainstorm, or compose

- **Learning**: guiding you through new skills, topics, or languages

- **Collaboration**: mediating teamwork or offering project management support

In this sense, your AI isn't just a critic. It's a **co-creator**, always in your corner.

Risks and Ethical Design

There are real dangers here:

- Overdependence on AI could reduce human initiative or social interaction

- Poorly trained models could reflect cultural or ideological bias

- Companions could become echo chambers if not designed to challenge

- Vulnerable users might anthropomorphize or over-trust their AI

These risks demand **strict ethical oversight**, diverse training data, and **robust mental health partnerships**.

AI should augment human flourishing—not simulate intimacy in place of it.

The Future of Social Media Is Conversational

We're entering a world where you no longer just post and scroll—you **interact, explore, and reflect** in dialogue with intelligent systems.

This shift, if handled wisely, could **reintroduce depth, reflection, and self-awareness** to the social web.

It could make us **better thinkers**, not just faster scrollers.
Better citizens. Better listeners.
More grounded. More connected.

And it all starts with a simple idea:
Let AI be your companion—not your controller.

In the next chapter, we move beyond the individual experience to tackle a larger social challenge: **designing for healthy public dialogue**. How do we redesign comment sections, discussion threads, and online communities to prioritize civility, understanding, and collective wisdom?

Let's find out.

Chapter 6: Designing for Healthy Dialogue

Scroll through any comment section today and you'll see it:
A shouting match.
Snark over substance.
Performative rage.
Misunderstanding turned viral.

Once envisioned as digital town squares, social media platforms have instead become arenas—where reasoned dialogue is drowned out by noise, and the loudest voices dominate.

But it doesn't have to be this way.

In this chapter, we reimagine **conversation architecture** for the Age of AI. We explore how platforms can promote **constructive dialogue** over confrontation, and how technology can help us listen better, think deeper, and **rediscover the power of public conversation**.

The Problem With Comments Today

The comment section—once a place for engagement—is now often a **battlefield**. Why?

- **Noisy hierarchies**: Comments are sorted by upvotes or recency, not quality.

- **Mob dynamics**: A small group can dominate the tone and direction of a thread.

- **Performative incentives**: Users speak to win likes, not to understand others.

- **Lack of context**: Replies often ignore the nuance or intention of the original post.

- **Trolls and bad-faith actors**: Civility becomes collateral damage.

The result? **Polarization, burnout, and disengagement.**

Dialogue as a Designed System

What if we designed digital conversations with the same care we give to great classrooms, town halls, or mediation circles?

In the Age of AI, we can.

Core Principles of Healthy Dialogue Design

1. **Civility by Default**
   Design defaults that set a respectful tone. Examples:

   - Comment boxes that prompt: "What question might deepen this conversation?"

- Emojis that reward kindness or insight, not just outrage.

2. **Contextual Clarity**

   - Highlight the original claim or question in any thread.

   - Allow users to annotate their intent (e.g., "asking," "challenging," "adding personal experience").

3. **Visibility for Constructive Voices**

   - Use AI to rank comments by **thoughtfulness**, **empathy**, or **factual clarity**—not just likes.

   - Surface user contributions that bridge divides, not widen them.

4. **De-escalation Tools**

   - AI can detect rising emotional tension and suggest a pause, paraphrase, or reframing prompt.

   - Conflict-aware bots could propose common ground statements when threads get heated.

5. **Slow Commenting Mode**

   - Time-gated replies encourage reflection.

   - Users are nudged to read the entire post before replying.

   - Limit reactive posting with cooldown timers.

6. **Conversation Summaries**

   - At the top of every long thread, AI offers a summary of key points and agreements/disagreements.

- ○ Optional "TL;DR" previews make long discussions more accessible.

7. **Community Moderation, Not Censorship**

   - ○ Empower trusted users to guide discussions—not just flag violations.

   - ○ Create roles like "dialogue hosts" or "topic editors" drawn from the community.

Reimagining Replies, Reactions, and Threads

What if "reply" wasn't the default action? What if users were encouraged to **ask a question**, **build upon an idea**, or **offer a related link** instead?

What if reactions weren't limited to likes or anger, but included:

- 💬 "This made me think"

- ✊ "I have a question"

- 💡 "This connects to something else"

- ✳ "This helped complete my understanding"

By **broadening expressive tools**, we shift interaction from judgment to collaboration.

Conversational Spaces, Not Just Feeds

Instead of treating comments as clutter beneath posts, we can elevate them into **dynamic conversational spaces**:

- Dedicated threads with optional facilitation by AI or community guides

- Visual maps of dialogue trees showing branching ideas

- Topic-based salons where users gather around shared curiosities, not controversies

These spaces become **arenas of synthesis** rather than arenas of conflict.

AI as Dialogue Steward

In this redesigned system, AI serves not as a censor but as a **conversation steward**:

- Recommending better phrasing

- Detecting when people are talking past each other

- Suggesting questions to unblock stuck dialogues

- Surfacing complementary ideas from other threads or communities

It's like having a skilled moderator or dialectic coach embedded in every conversation.

Empowering Digital Citizenship

To make this work, we must also cultivate a **culture of digital civics**:

- Reward users not just for volume, but for contribution quality

- Offer in-platform "dialogue literacy" badges and learning modules

- Let users build reputations as bridge-builders, not just content creators

This is how we shift from "engagement economy" to **conversation economy**—where thoughtfulness has real value.

From Comment Sections to Civic Commons

Done right, conversation systems can become the **new civic infrastructure**:

- Places where complex problems are unpacked

- Where disagreement sharpens understanding

- Where people from different backgrounds meet—not to perform, but to **learn**

In a world where attention is cheap but understanding is rare, this shift could be revolutionary.

A Better Way to Talk

What if the internet made us more articulate?
More open-minded?
More able to disagree with grace?

With the right design, it can.

Social networks shouldn't amplify noise. They should **amplify dialogue**. In the Age of AI, that's not just possible—it's imperative.

In the next chapter, we tackle one of the deepest problems facing digital society: **the echo chamber**. How can we break free from filter bubbles and algorithmic silos—and build a social web that **challenges**, **expands**, and **diversifies** our thinking?

Let's find out.

Chapter 7: Escaping the Echo Chamber

We were promised a global village.
 Instead, we got a labyrinth of echo chambers.

One of the most pernicious effects of algorithmically driven social media has been the **narrowing of worldviews**. Over time, the content we see is tailored to our preferences, biases, fears, and beliefs—until we are surrounded by a digital mirror that reflects only ourselves.

This phenomenon is not just isolating; it's dangerous. It creates polarization, weakens democratic debate, and fuels radicalization. In the worst cases, it becomes a petri dish for extremism.

This chapter explores how a social network built for the Age of AI can break that cycle—and **open the windows of the mind**, not just polish its mirrors.

What Is an Echo Chamber?

An **echo chamber** is an environment where:

- You are only exposed to views that align with your own

- Contradictory voices are excluded, mocked, or algorithmically suppressed

- Reinforcement of belief is rewarded more than exploration of alternatives

It's not always intentional. It's the result of:

- **Engagement-based algorithms** that show you what you already agree with

- **Social pressures** that discourage dissent

- **Cognitive bias** (especially confirmation bias and motivated reasoning)

The longer you stay in one, the more your views harden—and the less tolerant you become of those who disagree.

The Filter Bubble Effect

Coined by Eli Pariser in 2011, the **filter bubble** refers to algorithmic personalization that insulates users from opposing viewpoints.

The result:

- Liberals and conservatives get different headlines.

- Different scientific "truths" circulate in different groups.

- People live in separate realities—often unaware those differences even exist.

This isn't just about politics. Filter bubbles also affect views on health, climate, religion, history, and culture.

Why Breaking the Bubble Matters

When people are exposed only to reinforcing narratives, the social fabric frays. Consequences include:

- **Political extremism**

- **Erosion of shared facts**

- **Mutual incomprehension**

- **Breakdown of empathy**

In a diverse, democratic society, we don't need to agree on everything—but we must **at least understand what others believe** and why.

That begins with designing systems that **intentionally disrupt the echo chamber.**

Toward Algorithmic Diversity

A next-gen social platform can use AI not to entrench your worldview—but to **challenge and expand it**.

Here's how:

▪ Worldview Mode Selector

Let users toggle how much ideological variety they want. Options could include:

- **Comfort Me**: Prioritize familiar perspectives

- **Balance Me**: Offer a mix of familiar and divergent views

- **Challenge Me**: Prioritize thoughtful, well-sourced counterpoints

- **Surprise Me**: Show content from random or global perspectives

This gives control back to users, but **nudges growth over time**.

💣 Diverse Content Paths

When a user reads an article or watches a video, AI can offer:

- "Here's how people from other political views see this"

- "Want to explore opposing perspectives?"

- "Here's a timeline of how this issue evolved over time"

These paths aren't confrontational—they're **invitational**.

🧠 Cognitive Contrast Prompts

Imagine your AI companion saying:

> "This article made a strong case. Want to see a well-argued counterpoint?"
> "You've seen 10 similar posts—want to switch gears?"

Gentle nudges. Big effects.

Exposure Without Exploitation

It's not enough to simply inject opposing views.
 Context and quality matter.

Unfiltered exposure can backfire—especially if it's:

- Trollish

- Mocking

- Poorly argued

Instead, the system must prioritize **respectful, high-quality dissent**—the kind that teaches, not provokes.

AI can help by:

- Filtering for **good-faith disagreement**

- Ranking sources based on credibility and tone

- Annotating key contrasts and shared assumptions

The goal isn't to convert, but to **enrich**.

Globalizing the Feed

Most feeds are not just ideological silos—they're **cultural silos**.

A truly expansive platform can offer:

- **Geo-cultural perspective layering** ("Here's how users in Ghana, Germany, and Indonesia are responding to this issue")

- **Translation AI** to bring global insights into your local context

- **Cross-border debates** facilitated by shared AI moderators

This helps create **global empathy**, not just global noise.

Echo Chamber Diagnostics

What if your AI assistant showed you a dashboard like this:

- 87% of your viewed content comes from left-leaning sources

- You've seen 0 perspectives from conservative economists this month

- 95% of your interactions are with people under age 30

Not as criticism—but as insight.
To help you ask: **Is this the intellectual ecosystem I want to live in?**

Reputational Tools for Bridge Builders

Incentives matter.

Platforms should reward—not punish—those who:

- Offer respectful counterpoints

- Ask clarifying questions

- Link across ideological silos

- Participate in cross-perspective dialogues

Imagine a **"Bridge Builder" badge** or **reputation score** based on how constructively you engage across divides.

Escaping the Echo Chamber Is a Choice

We cannot force people out of their filters.
 But we can **build platforms that invite, reward, and normalize openness**.

In the Age of AI, this is more than just an ethical goal—it's a survival necessity. Societies need shared facts, mutual understanding, and open dialogue to endure.

The echo chamber was the default design of the last internet.

Let the **next internet be designed for discovery.**

In the next chapter, we turn to another critical tension in online life: **identity**. How can we balance real-world verification with the need for pseudonymity, privacy, and safe expression?

The future of the internet depends on how we handle **who we are online**.

Chapter 8: Identity in the Digital Age

Who are you online?

Are you the person behind your real name, verified and traceable?
 Or are you the pseudonym who feels safer speaking freely, testing ideas, or simply escaping judgment?

In the digital world, **identity is both a key and a shield**. It grants access, builds trust, and authenticates truth—but it also protects privacy, enables dissent, and gives voice to the vulnerable.

In the Age of AI, where impersonation is easy and misinformation rampant, the question of **digital identity** becomes one of the most important—and one of the most complex.

This chapter explores how a next-generation social network can balance **verification and anonymity**, **safety and authenticity**, **freedom and accountability**—not by choosing one or the other, but by **designing intelligently for both.**

The Crisis of Identity Online

The legacy internet was built on anonymity. Early forums, chatrooms, and platforms like Reddit encouraged pseudonymous participation. This enabled creativity, vulnerability, and experimentation—but also harassment, impersonation, and manipulation.

As the internet became more mainstream, platforms like Facebook pushed real-name policies. The idea was that **authentic identity leads to accountability**.

But that wasn't always true. Real names didn't stop abuse. And they exposed marginalized users to surveillance, discrimination, and real-world harm.

Then came AI.

Suddenly, anyone could:

- Clone voices

- Generate fake faces

- Forge credentials

- Create armies of bot accounts at scale

The result: a new kind of identity crisis—**too many identities**, all unverified, some malicious, many untraceable.

We need a new model.

The Case for Verified Identity

Some spaces online **require authenticity**:

- Civic discussions (e.g., voting policy, public forums)

- Journalism and fact-based debates

- Financial transactions or legal declarations

- Professional or scientific collaboration

In these cases, **real identity builds trust**. You know who you're talking to. Claims can be contextualized. Reputations can be earned.

A next-gen network should offer **Verified Identity Zones**, where:

- Users are required to complete identity verification

- Real names or known professional aliases are used

- Content is moderated to higher standards

- AI bot detection runs continuously

These zones could be opt-in spaces for **deliberation, collaboration, and decision-making**—like digital versions of the public square.

The Case for Pseudonymity

But not everyone wants—or should be forced—to use their real name.

Pseudonymity is essential for:

- Whistleblowers and political dissidents

- Victims of abuse seeking support

- People exploring stigmatized identities or ideas

- Young users who are still forming their sense of self

- Artists, thinkers, and creators who wish to separate their work from their legal identity

Pseudonymity isn't the enemy of truth. When well-designed, it can **enhance authenticity**, by allowing people to say what they truly believe, free from fear.

A future-proof platform should preserve **Pseudonymous Expression Zones**, where:

- Users can build verified reputations without revealing their real name

- Moderation focuses on behavior, not identity

- AI ensures one person = one account (Sybil resistance), without violating privacy

- Identity is **persistent, accountable, and consent-based**, even if it's not public

This allows freedom **without chaos**.

Sybil Resistance and AI Bot Detection

One of the biggest threats to online identity today is **fake accounts**—bots, trolls, or malicious actors using hundreds of profiles to manipulate discourse.

AI offers powerful tools to detect:

- Linguistic patterns of bots

- Coordinated behavior across accounts

- Fake images or identity documents

- Voiceprint and biometric fraud

A future platform must include **real-time AI bot detection**—running continuously in the background to flag suspicious activity, verify account uniqueness, and protect genuine users.

This isn't just moderation—it's **identity hygiene**.

Progressive Identity Architecture

Here's a better model: **Progressive Identity**.

- On signup, users can choose their **identity level**: pseudonymous, semi-anonymous, or verified

- They can **upgrade** or **downgrade** their visibility at any time

- Different zones of the platform require different levels of verification

- Identity is **modular**: you can verify just enough to participate, without overexposing yourself

- AI ensures **authentic behavior**, even without full identity disclosure

This offers **flexibility, safety, and control**—especially important in a world of constant surveillance and AI-powered doxxing.

Digital Reputation Without Real Names

Reputation is the bedrock of trust—but it doesn't require your passport.

New systems can allow users to build **reputation scores** based on:

- Accuracy of shared information

- Constructiveness in dialogue

- Contributions to the community

- Peer reviews or upvotes

- Longevity and consistency of identity

This means even pseudonymous users can earn trust, authority, and visibility.

In a well-designed system, **behavior becomes identity**—not branding, not bragging, not personal data.

Identity and Consent

One of the greatest violations of trust in today's internet is the **non-consensual extraction of identity**:

- Data scraping

- Deepfake impersonation

- Facial recognition without consent

- Surveillance capitalism

A new network must reverse that paradigm. Identity should always be:

- **User-owned**

- **Consensually shared**

- **Portable across platforms**

- **Protected by encryption and policy**

This is where decentralized identity tools (like **DIDs**, **verifiable credentials**, and **blockchain wallets**) can offer real value—**not to tokenize people**, but to empower them.

The Future: Plural Identity, Singular Integrity

You may have multiple digital selves: a real-name professional, a pseudonymous activist, an anonymous artist.

That's not fragmentation—it's **pluralism**. Just like in the real world, where we speak differently at home, at work, and in a protest march.

The goal isn't to force all identity into one mold.
 The goal is to ensure that all identity—**however expressed**—is treated with dignity, protected with care, and empowered to participate meaningfully in public life.

In the Age of AI, identity must be **fluid, secure, and ethical**.

In the next chapter, we look beneath the surface—to the very foundations of the social network itself. What kind of infrastructure—technical, institutional, and ethical—can sustain a platform designed for truth, trust, and democracy?

Let's dig into **infrastructure for integrity.**

Chapter 9: Infrastructure for Integrity

Modern social media platforms are often built like casinos: closed systems optimized for manipulation, not meaning. Under the hood, their infrastructure is proprietary, opaque, and designed to extract maximum engagement and data with minimal accountability.

But if we're going to reimagine the social network for the Age of AI—where trust is scarce and truth is contested—we need to think differently. We need to **build it like a public utility, not a digital slot machine**.

This chapter explores the **technical and ethical infrastructure** necessary to support a new kind of platform—one designed not just to scale, but to **earn trust, protect democracy, and enhance the public good.**

Why Infrastructure Matters

When people talk about social networks, they often focus on **what they see**—the posts, the feeds, the comments. But the real power lies **beneath the surface**:

- The codebase that decides what's shown

- The databases that collect your behavior

- The moderation tools that filter speech

- The business model that drives everything

If these foundations are flawed, no design feature can fix them. That's why integrity must be **built into the infrastructure**, not bolted on afterward.

Principle #1: Open Architecture, Not Black Boxes

Today's platforms are black boxes. Their algorithms, data flows, and moderation decisions are hidden from public view.

A next-gen network must adopt **open architecture**, which includes:

- **Transparent algorithms**: Users can see how feeds are ranked, or choose from different ranking models

- **Open APIs**: Developers can build tools, extensions, and overlays

- **Auditable moderation logs**: Key decisions can be reviewed by independent watchdogs

- **Open-source components**: Core logic can be inspected by the public and improved by the community

This doesn't mean giving up security. It means **inviting trust through visibility**.

Principle #2: Decentralization with Purpose

Decentralization is not a magic wand—but when done right, it can support:

- **Resilience**: No single point of failure or censorship

- **Local governance**: Communities can set their own rules, norms, and culture

- **User ownership**: Data belongs to individuals, not platforms

- **Interoperability**: Different apps can talk to each other using common protocols

This could look like a **federated model** (think: Mastodon), where a central protocol powers many local instances—or a **Web3 model**, where identity and data live in user-controlled wallets, not corporate servers.

The key is balance: decentralization that enhances **freedom and accountability**, not just fragmentation.

Principle #3: Governance Beyond Corporations

Infrastructure needs governance. The current model—private boards making opaque decisions under shareholder pressure—is insufficient.

A better system includes:

- **Multistakeholder governance**: Developers, users, moderators, ethicists, and regulators all have a seat at the table

- **Citizen ethics councils**: Randomly selected users review hard content decisions and algorithmic changes

- **Constitutional principles**: A written framework guides how rights, moderation, and innovation are handled

- **Public reporting requirements**: Regular transparency reports show what's being taken down, flagged, or promoted—and why

This shifts the platform from a **tech monopoly** to a **civic platform**.

Principle #4: Data Dignity and Portability

Data is not oil. It's the **digital trail of your life**—and it deserves protection.

The platform should support:

- **Data portability**: You can leave the network, take your data, and go elsewhere

- **Data minimization**: Only essential data is collected—no surveillance by default

- **Encrypted messaging and private zones**

- **Monetization on your terms**: If your data is used commercially, you share in the value

In other words, **you control your identity, your attention, and your contributions.**

Principle #5: Built-in Moderation Tools—But with Checks and Balances

Moderation is infrastructure. It must be fast, fair, and scalable—but also **subject to appeal, transparency, and revision.**

AI can play a powerful role in first-line moderation:

- Flagging hate speech, doxxing, impersonation, and spam

- Surfacing risky or emotionally volatile threads for human review

- Supporting community-driven standards across zones

But final decisions—especially on gray areas—should rest with **trusted, accountable humans**, not automated systems.

Principle #6: Ethical Revenue Models

A platform built on advertising will always prioritize **engagement over integrity**. That's a conflict of interest hardwired into the system.

New infrastructure requires new incentives. Viable models include:

- **Subscription tiers**: Free access + premium features

- **Creator economy**: Tip jars, micropayments, and monetized contributions

- **Public interest funding**: Grants for platforms that serve democratic or educational goals

- **AI services**: Paid access to advanced AI tools, not behavioral data

Revenue must align with user value—not attention extraction.

Building for Global Equity

Much of the world is still coming online. A platform for the future must consider:

- **Low-bandwidth usability**

- **Multilingual accessibility**

- **Local moderation in cultural context**

- **Zero-rating or subsidized access in developing countries**

- **Offline features** for unstable connections

This ensures the platform is not just **by design ethical**, but **by default inclusive.**

Infrastructure as a Public Good

What if we treated social infrastructure the way we treat water, roads, or libraries?

- Something we all rely on

- Something that shapes daily life

- Something that must be built to last, not just to profit

In this model, the platform becomes **part of the civic fabric**—subject to scrutiny, co-designed with communities, protected against capture, and stewarded for generations.

This doesn't mean banning private companies from building social tools. But it means **setting foundational rules that serve people, not profit margins.**

A New Foundation

If trust is the currency of the future internet, then **integrity is the architecture**.

We need to build networks that:

- Are transparent by design

- Are accountable by structure

- Are ethical by incentive

- Are inclusive by intention

This is no small task. But infrastructure, once built right, can **scale truth, not just reach**. It can foster solidarity, not just virality. It can become the silent strength behind everything else.

And that brings us to our next step: the money. In the next chapter, we'll explore **monetization without manipulation**—how to fund this new network without compromising its soul.

Chapter 10: Monetizing Without Manipulation

Every social network must answer one simple question:
How does it survive?

The business model of a platform isn't just an afterthought. It **shapes everything**—from its interface to its ethics, from what gets promoted to what gets hidden. And for most of the past two decades, social media has run on one dominant business model:

Surveillance capitalism.

Users are not the customers. They're the product. Advertisers are the real clients. And the currency is your attention—captured, packaged, and sold.

This model has led to an internet optimized not for **truth**, **well-being**, or **growth**—but for **addiction**, **polarization**, and **manipulation**.

In this chapter, we imagine something better: a platform where revenue doesn't come at the cost of reality. Where monetization is aligned with value creation—not value extraction.

The Attention Economy Is Broken

Let's look at what's gone wrong:

- **Clickbait wins** because more views = more revenue

- **Misinformation thrives** because falsehoods are more engaging

- **Algorithms are weaponized** to hijack emotion and outrage

- **User data is harvested** with little consent and sold with less transparency

- **Creators chase virality**, not depth, because the system only rewards scale

In short: the financial incentives of today's platforms **corrupt the very purpose** of social media—connection, dialogue, and discovery.

To build a better future, we need to shift from an **attention-based economy** to a **value-based economy**.

Core Principle: Align Monetization With Integrity

In the new model, the question is not "What keeps people online?" but:

- What **helps them grow**?

- What content or interaction **enriches the community**?

- What services or tools do people **value enough to support financially**?

The goal is to **fund the platform without undermining its soul**.

Revenue Streams That Respect the User

Here are models that monetize **without manipulation**:

💡 1. Premium Subscriptions

- Free core features for everyone

- Paid tiers unlock tools like:

    - Advanced AI companions

    - Private communities

    - Creative publishing tools

    - Advanced analytics or customization

- Subscribers support the platform **directly**, not through data exploitation

This model aligns with user loyalty, not user addiction.

💬 2. Creator Economy & Micropayments

- Users can **tip**, **sponsor**, or **subscribe** to their favorite thinkers and creators

- Content with high civic or educational value can be **rewarded by the crowd**

- Micropayment systems allow **a few cents per insight**, frictionlessly

Incentivizes **quality over quantity**.

⚫ 3. Public-Interest Funding

- Governments, foundations, and academic institutions can **fund infrastructure** that promotes civic engagement, literacy, or democratic participation

- Think of it like **PBS for the digital age**

Especially important in non-commercial or underserved contexts.

4. AI-as-a-Service

- Advanced tools—like research assistants, writing helpers, visual AI, or translation engines—can be monetized

- Power users pay for premium models

- Entry-level services remain free or subsidized

AI becomes a **toolset, not a trick**.

5. Privacy-Respecting Sponsorships

- Ethical ads, served **contextually** rather than behaviorally

- No microtargeting, no surveillance

- Sponsors pay to be **part of a trusted information environment**, not to hijack it

Ads are **transparent, relevant, and unobtrusive**.

Rewarding the Right Kind of Engagement

To avoid the mistakes of the attention economy, the platform must **redefine success metrics**:

Instead of:

- Time spent

- Clicks

- Shares

Use:

- **Insight gained**

- **Constructive contribution**

- **Reputation earned**

- **Community impact**

In other words, the most "valuable" content isn't what goes viral—it's what **elevates the dialogue**.

AI can help score, surface, and reward this type of contribution.

Creators, Not Influencers

In the current system, "influencer" has become synonymous with **manipulation**: curating personas for likes, selling attention to brands, chasing algorithmic favor.

A better system nurtures **creators**, thinkers, and bridge-builders by:

- Giving them tools to **earn** without selling out

- Letting them own their **audience data and distribution**

- Offering **shared revenue** for content that teaches, builds, or connects

This is how we move from performative content to **meaningful work**.

Community-Owned Models

Some platforms could go further and embrace **cooperative ownership**:

- Users or creators can **own shares** in the platform

- Governance decisions (like algorithm updates or moderation rules) are voted on

- Profits are reinvested or distributed transparently

This model fosters a deeper sense of **responsibility and alignment**.

Avoiding the Trap of Tokenomics

Web3 advocates often propose token-based economies. While promising in theory, tokenomics can:

- Incentivize spam and speculation

- Create economic inequality within the platform

- Turn every interaction into a transaction

If used, tokens should serve **utility**, not hype—enabling access, identity, or collaboration—not endless gamification.

Reimagining Ads: Transparency and Choice

If advertising must exist, it must be:

- **Opt-in**: Users choose whether to see ads

- **Non-extractive**: No tracking, no profiling, no behavioral data harvesting

- **Relevant by context**, not by surveillance

- **Respectful**: No auto-play, no dark patterns

And users should have the option to **pay to remove ads entirely.**

Ethical Monetization Is a Design Challenge

It's easy to say "don't be evil." It's harder to **design systems where being good is more profitable than being manipulative.**

But it is possible.

By aligning revenue with value, behavior with contribution, and data with dignity, we can build a social network that sustains itself **without cannibalizing our trust, time, and attention.**

In the next chapter, we go from infrastructure to innovation—exploring **how a new kind of social network can evolve in real-time**, through experimentation, reflection, and continuous ethical improvement.

Welcome to **Civic Labs and Ethical Experimentation**.

Chapter 11: Civic Labs and Ethical Experimentation

No platform, no matter how well-designed, will get everything right the first time.

Social networks are not static structures—they are **living systems**, shaped by evolving norms, unpredictable behaviors, and emergent challenges. The difference between platforms that grow ethically and those that decay is not perfection—it's **responsiveness**.

In this chapter, we explore how a next-generation network can embed **experimentation, iteration, and ethical reflection** into its very DNA—turning the platform into a **Civic Lab**, where users help test, refine, and co-create the future of digital society.

Why Social Networks Must Evolve

The internet is a dynamic, unpredictable space. What works today may backfire tomorrow. A feature designed for safety might be misused for censorship. A ranking tweak meant to promote fairness might accidentally suppress creativity.

We've seen this repeatedly:

- Comment upvotes promoting mob mentality

- Real-name policies silencing vulnerable voices

- Trending topics amplifying fringe ideas

- Auto-suggestions fueling conspiracy loops

The takeaway? Even small design decisions can **reshape public discourse**.

That's why the future social network must move beyond static policy and become **an experimental civic space**—a digital democracy lab that learns, adapts, and grows with its users.

What Is a Civic Lab?

A **Civic Lab** is a structured environment within the platform where:

- New features, policies, or moderation tools can be tested

- Experiments are opt-in and transparent

- Users receive clear feedback about what's being tested and why

- Outcomes are shared publicly to promote accountability and learning

Think of it as an **open-source R&D wing for democracy and dialogue**, built into the heart of the platform.

What Could Be Tested?

1. **Comment System Variants**

   - Do time-delayed replies reduce hostility?

   - Does hiding usernames improve content quality?

   - Can AI-suggested rephrasings foster empathy?

2. **Feed Algorithms**

   - Do diversity-enhancing feeds reduce polarization?

   - What happens when users can choose their algorithmic lens?

3. **Fact-Checking Tools**

   - How do different kinds of truth overlays affect user trust?

   - Does collaborative fact-checking outperform centralized models?

4. **Reputation and Reward Systems**

   - Can positive contribution scores reduce trolling?

   - Do peer-nominated "community leaders" improve discourse?

5. **Conflict De-escalation Prompts**

   - Can AI detect rising tension and offer calming cues?

   - Does visualizing shared values change the course of heated debates?

These aren't just tech features—they're **experiments in public culture.**

Designing Ethical Experiments

Ethical experimentation must follow **clear guardrails**:

- **Informed consent**: Users opt in, with full understanding of what's being tested

- **Right to exit**: Users can leave an experiment at any time

- **No manipulation**: Users are never deceived or nudged without awareness

- **Independent oversight**: An ethics board reviews proposed experiments

- **Public transparency**: Results are shared, even when they fail

This builds **trust in experimentation**, making users **co-designers**, not test subjects.

User Participation and Feedback Loops

The Civic Lab model empowers users to:

- **Propose experiments**

- **Vote on which features to test**

- **Join cross-community pilot groups**

- **Access dashboards** showing how design changes affect their experience

Imagine a weekly Civic Lab update:

> "This week, 20,000 users tested a 'question-only' comment mode. Troll activity dropped by 42%. Next week, we're testing community-curated discussion prompts."

The network becomes a **co-created commons**, evolving with shared insight.

A/B Testing for the Public Good

While A/B testing is common in tech, it's usually **secretive and profit-driven**. In a Civic Lab, A/B testing is:

- Openly declared

- Designed with social impact in mind

- Reviewed for unintended consequences

- Focused on **dialogue quality**, **user trust**, and **civic learning**

This transforms testing from exploitation to **exploration**.

Learning from Public Infrastructure

Cities test traffic patterns, school curricula, and zoning laws. Democracies test voting systems and public health campaigns. The Civic Lab takes that same spirit and applies it to **digital society**.

Instead of rigid rules, it offers **living frameworks**, updated with new data, feedback, and cultural shifts.

Rapid Response to Harm

In a dynamic world, crises happen. The Civic Lab can serve as a **crisis response unit**, rapidly deploying:

- New moderation protocols for emerging harms

- Emergency adjustments to prevent mass disinformation

- Safe spaces for affected communities

- Public updates on what's being done and why

This replaces opaque PR with **accountable action**.

Institutional Memory and Iteration

Most platforms forget. They repeat mistakes. They swing between extremes—over-policing, then under-policing; promoting openness, then suppressing dissent.

A Civic Lab maintains a **living archive of experiments**, with:

- What was tested

- What worked

- What failed

- Why decisions were made

This creates **institutional memory**, helping the platform **grow wiser over time.**

Culture of Curiosity, Not Control

At its heart, the Civic Lab fosters a new culture—where users are:

- Curious, not combative

- Engaged, not exploited

- Empowered, not engineered

It turns **users into citizens**, and the network into **a laboratory for democracy**.

The Platform That Evolves With You

The Civic Lab transforms the network from a product into a **process**.

It says:

> "We don't know all the answers. But we're building this with you—openly, iteratively, ethically."

And in an era of declining institutional trust, that may be the most radical innovation of all.

In the final chapter, we step back to look at the bigger picture: a future where technology doesn't just avoid harm, but **actively fosters peace, empathy, and human flourishing.**

Let's close this journey with a vision worth pursuing.

Chapter 12: A Peace Worth Pursuing

We began with a question:
What would a social network look like if it were built for the Age of AI—not to manipulate us, but to **elevate us**?

We've answered it piece by piece: truth layers, AI companions, dialogue redesigns, identity architecture, ethical monetization, civic labs. But all of this has been in service of something deeper:

A vision of peace—not as silence or avoidance, but as **the outcome of shared understanding**, mutual respect, and civic trust.

Because social networks are no longer just platforms. They are **invisible institutions**, shaping how we think, speak, and relate. And in a time of deep division, rampant misinformation, and weaponized technology, what they amplify—or suppress—can determine the very future of democracy, community, and global harmony.

This final chapter is a call to remember:
Peace is not the absence of noise. It is the presence of design that dignifies the human voice.

The Possibility of Peace

Peace, in the context of social technology, means:

- A place where **disagreement is possible** without dehumanization

- A system that encourages **reflection before reaction**

- Tools that help us see one another not as enemies, but as **complex human beings**

- An architecture that supports **truthful, constructive, and inclusive dialogue**

- A culture where listening is as valued as speaking

It means a network that doesn't just reduce harm—it actively cultivates **understanding**.

The Role of AI

The arrival of AI presents both a threat and an opportunity.

Used irresponsibly, it can deepen echo chambers, turbocharge propaganda, and simulate reality to the point of erasure.

But used with care, intention, and ethics, AI can become:

- A **co-pilot for truth**

- A **mediator in conflict**

- A **translator across cultures**

- A **companion in learning**

- A **protector of the vulnerable**

- A **magnifier of our better selves**

AI doesn't have to replace us. It can **remind us who we want to be**.

From Platforms to Ecosystems

The future of social technology is not in a single app or feed. It's in **ecosystems** of connected tools, shared protocols, and civic values. Networks that are:

- **Federated**, not monopolized

- **Transparent**, not manipulative

- **Collaborative**, not extractive

- **Diverse**, not homogenized

- **Democratic**, not authoritarian

In this ecosystem, no one company controls the narrative. No single algorithm defines what is true. Instead, we co-create digital spaces that reflect **pluralism, accountability, and compassion**.

Toward a Digital Commons

The greatest mistake of Web 2.0 was building the public square on private servers.

The next era must reclaim social media as a form of **digital commons**—not owned by billionaires, but **stewarded by citizens**, communities, and ethical technologists.

That will require new laws, new institutions, new incentives—and most of all, **new imagination**.

The Builders of Peace

This is a call to:

- **Designers**, to craft humane interfaces and dignity-first systems

- **Engineers**, to write code that protects rather than exploits

- **Entrepreneurs**, to prove that ethical products can scale

- **Educators**, to teach digital literacy as a core civic skill

- **Governments**, to regulate with wisdom, not reaction

- **Communities**, to model better norms and mentor each other

- **Artists**, to imagine the unseen and inspire the possible

- **Users**, to engage with intention, empathy, and curiosity

The future won't be handed to us.
It will be built—by people who care.

A Vision Worth Pursuing

Let us imagine a social network that doesn't divide, addict, or deceive—but one that helps us become **better versions of ourselves**.

A place where:

- Truth has scaffolding

- Dissent has dignity

- Peace isn't passive—it's engineered

A place that recognizes that technology alone won't save us—**but how we shape it just might**.

Because the real revolution isn't in machine learning.
 It's in human learning—rediscovering how to speak, listen, think, and coexist in a world that feels like it's falling apart.

Let's build something better.
 Let's build a network of peace.

www.ingramcontent.com/pod-product-compliance
Lightning Source LLC
LaVergne TN
LVHW080118070326
832902LV00015B/2660